It's Time...

to be cool

How Awareness and Insight can Make You Calm and Confident

Aruna Ladva

BKIS

Brahma Kumaris

Inspired Stillness

IT'S TIME ... TO BE COOL
How Awareness and Insight can Make You Calm and Confident
Aruna Ladva

PRINT ISBN 978-1-886872-79-0
KINDLE ISBN 978-1-886872-80-6
EPUB ISBN 978-1-886872-81-3

First published in 2016 by Brahma Kumaris Information Services Ltd, Global Co-operation House, 65 Pound Lane, London, NW10 2HH
Website: www.inspiredstillness.com
E-mail: enquiries@bkpublications.com

Illustrations by kind courtesy Mr Joachim Debarge.
Designed by Webspeed Ltd, Colchester
Printed In India by Imprint Digital Ltd.

It is said that nowadays people have hot heads and cold hearts; what we need to do is turn that around; we need to have cool minds and warm hearts.

BK Jayanti

Contents

Introduction

It's becoming increasingly clear that the heat and tension in our world is rising day by day. It is revealing itself in our personal and professional lives, in politics and in global events.

There is a great need at this time to stay calm and composed; physically, mentally and emotionally. If we simply carry on reacting to conflicts and challenges in a negative or misguided way, we are adding fuel to the fire.

In this fourth book, Aruna again offers new and sometimes surprising perspectives on dealing with everyday challenges. As one who sincerely seeks change, Aruna writes from the heart, as well as from her experience of approaching and experimenting with life from the inside out.

She plays on the word 'cool', but the underlying state of being that she is inviting us to invoke for ourselves is that of being calm, free from tension, and free from overwhelming emotions that impair our judgements.

Coolness in a spiritual sense is something that comes from contemplating the deeper aspects of life, from knowing and understanding ourselves better, and from drawing upon the deep wellspring of wisdom that is within all of us.

With a cool mind and a clear intellect we can learn to thoughtfully respond to situations, and begin to operate less from conditioned responses and more from positive feelings and intentions.

This book offers many insights on how to manage our minds and manage our lives better. It teaches us how to dissolve anger and to create inner silence, how to slow down and appreciate life, and how to become internally strong.

Take your time in reading this book. Use it as a catalyst for your own deeper contemplation, and then go back into the world cool, calm and refreshed.

By Carol Lipthorpe

Aware & Insightful

Are You Smarter Than Your Smart Phone?

Apparently there are about 6.8 billion cell phones in the world. That is just a little short of the total population of the world! One UN study shows that more people have cell phones than toilets! And chances are almost all of these subscribers will have their heads tucked in, bowing to their cell phones first thing in the morning, like it were a demi-god, enlightening them with its secrets. This ritual is hardly different from a worshiper who turns to God every morning for advice and insights. Yet at least the worshiper moves onto other things during the day, but for most of us, we stay glued to this 'light' all day.

As all of us dance to the tune of our cell phones, even in the literal sense, then we become out of tune with the magic of the moment. Just imagine how much we are missing as we engage our minds and bodies with that which is surreal and unnatural! We used to live in alignment with the sun and the moon, the natural elements, with people around us. We used to feel the breeze and the pulse of the town or city. Yet that is all long fading, as we get lured into the trap of this mystical, magical and magnetic gadget.

It seems old fashioned, almost prehistoric, not to own a cell phone. As for the addicts, they live in a different dimension, in an imaginative world, as they stay cemented to this 'brick' containing photos, music, games and videos. They live out their unfulfilled dream through Hollywood and Bollywood, Facebook and Face-time! Whilst the wonder of cell phones is that they have made far people close, they have also made the close ones far! As we lose our self in this

Pandora's box, we are not living in the moment, nor are we present with the one beside us. As soon as we get into the bus or the coffee shop, we dive into this glossy bubble of 'unreal' life. It is a form of escapism; our unwillingness to face our present reality or loneliness.

The downsides of using the cell phone are just as many as the miracles it promises. Multi-tasking is a myth and not as clever as one used to believe. The brain simply cannot switch from one activity to another whilst keeping its focus – no matter how smart(!) you may be. Cell phones are a great distraction and we are four times more likely to crash if we drive whilst using a cell phone, according to the USA Safety Council.

And, whilst we continue to drain the battery of the cell phone it is draining the battery of the mind at the same time. These electromagnetic frequencies are making people more sick by the day. No wonder that we do little, and yet feel more and more exhausted by the end of the day.

People answering calls that take precedence over prearranged appointments, is a very ill-mannered and disturbing habit that seems to be increasing by the day.

Use of cell phones, and the mastering of its apps would not be considered a very creative hobby. We are reacting more than responding, and we are hardly said to be using our initiative. It does not make use of the right, intuitive side of the brain. Young people are excelling at type chatting and texting, but developing fewer social skills, as they remain lost in their fantasy world. It's time to get off the thrill of that cyber skate-board and to get real.

Cell phones give us a false sense of security. We think we are safe with them and wouldn't be caught without them. Yet the more we rely on this technology with a limiting battery, we are not living in trust, but in fear. In fact our world may come crashing in when the battery crashes and this demi-god dies on us!

Cell phones are not altogether bad. They have their pluses and can even be educational if we are selective about how we use them. The question being raised here is, how much of a master am I, or is it mastering me?

It's Time… to get smarter than the smartphone! Don't allow it to rule your life!

More Haste, Less Speed

There is a very profound 'aha' moment when we realise that the more hastily we attempt and try to finish a task, then the less speedily we actually manage to accomplish it. In other words, the more we rush in order to cram more and more into our day, the less successful we become. We falter, and create more blunders, which then take extra time and energy to repair.

To be a fast thinker is a skill that is often rewarded in the workplace. However a mind that thinks too much and too fast without any control is like a car without any brakes. The saying goes: Power is nothing without control. This ambitious employee will succeed even more if he or she is able to apply a mental 'brake' when it is required.

Stop to ask yourself, what is the reason for your haste and hurry? Is the risk of speeding, in all senses of the word, really worth it? Speed only kills. Sometimes the person, the task, or the relationship, depending upon the circumstances.

How often have we said things in haste, only to regret them later, and perhaps over a long period of time – when a slight pause for thought might have saved that moment and more.

We hasten because we feel pressure, we feel we are losing control of our world, and therefore we attempt to get back on track: but often in a reckless and undisciplined way. Then the external results will not be orderly, as they will simply reflect the dis-orderly-ness within our minds.

It is because we are unable to control our thoughts, (which by the way, include all desires, ambitions, ideas, and other pursuance's) that we have little control over our lives. Reducing your thoughts is very much like reducing your to-do list. Wouldn't you feel relieved if you had a much shorter to-do list everyday?

In our haste, we want to try this, do that, fulfil the other, and we never really stop to look at the consequences or the effects of all these added pressures in our lives. When was the last time you took a review of your life? Is there any area that you can cut out or reduce to make things more relaxed, more manageable? You may find there are many!

The reason that we feel we need to rush through life is because there is a lot we want achieve. We also take on too much stress of living in a world that demands more and more from us. Are we perhaps expecting too much from ourselves and from the numbers on the clock? Be realistic, stay light, draw your boundaries, and slow down a little.

Slowing down does not imply being lazy, complacent or passive. But to take just a moment to step aside, to really breathe, is to increase self-respect by preventing this continuous self-damage caused by too much haste.

One of the profound lessons of meditation is that, as we slow down, we in fact 'create' more. Achieving more in deeds is one thing, and that is certain to happen, but to master thought energy is another thing altogether. As we deepen our meditation practice, we begin to experience that our thoughts can make things happen even from a distance.

We create a thought and it happens practically. We have another thought and that happens too! It's amazing!

As we become more and more in charge of our mind, we become more in charge of our life. We actually do less and become more. More efficient, more relaxed, more joyful, more successful and more fulfilled.

So now, put away those running shoes! No need to run away from or run after anything. By just sitting on your meditation chair you can take charge of your life and 'charge ahead'! Create the right internal environment and everything you need, will come to you at the right time. No haste, more speed!

It's Time… to slow down your thinking and speed up your successes! Put your internal 'house' in order, and reap the benefits of ease and flow, with much less effort!

Attitude of Gratitude

On a recent trip to southern Turkey, I had the experience of being suddenly plunged into darkness for a few hours only to find out later that a broken electricity cable had outed the electricity in the whole area. It was evening time in winter, so it was crucial to have some light and heat. It would also have been nice to have been able to make a cup of tea, cook dinner, and do some work on the internet, but all of that was out of the question! When I returned home to Kuwait expecting all to be 'normal' I found that we were out of running water because the pump had broken and the tank had not filled up. It was a double lesson from the 'drama of life' to remind me just how little we appreciate something – until it's not there!

And another interesting thing was… that even though I knew that there was no water or light, I still went, out of habit, to 'switch on' the lights and 'turn on' the taps! It's as though the mind was in denial refusing to accept the reality of the situation. It just shows how much we take for granted, and how much we assume that things will always be there at our disposal.

These incidents made me question: Am I appreciative about other things in my life? Having hot running water and electricity are important in our privileged modern day lives, but what about the ability to walk and move freely without pains and strains? Or to be able to see the world with our amazing eyesight? Or to be able to hear the world outside your window.

All of these things are so natural to us that we do not even think about them until they are not there. Only then do we lament.

When we begin to appreciate the beauty and richness of the treasures in front of and around us, then they take on a new and deeper meaning in our lives. There are so many aspects of nature to appreciate. If you can see some green grass and a few birds fluttering and singing, you are lucky – not everyone has this privilege. Hearing a running stream is also a privilege. Still better, if you are able to put your feet in it!

Changing the way we view the world around us, will change us, and change our world! It all begins with appreciating the little things in life.

There is a person who calls our meditation centre every day from prison. He has been an inmate for two years, and not a day has passed that he has not called for a chat and some positive thoughts. If I happen to answer his call it makes me so appreciative of the freedom of movement that I have. I admire so much that he stays happy and positive. He passes on these positive thoughts to others in the prison and creates motivational discussion forums! He is amazing! He has turned a negative situation into a positive one by just being grateful for what he has.

We can also be thankful for all the characters in our lives, the good, bad and the ugly. Each one is teaching us something. It's not a question here of thanking each person or each thing… just to be able to cultivate a consciousness of gratitude is enough. It's a state of mind, a way of being, a way of thinking. For example, even if you are held up in a queue you can be thankful for the opportunity to enjoy a few moments of tranquility.

Business Guru Steven Covey said, "We see the world, not as it is, but as we are..."

With so much apparently working against us in the world, and so much negativity in the news, we really need to make a list of all the good things that we have in our lives if we want to remain sane and happy. Once we are positive, we start sending positive energy out into the world, which then boomerangs back. The universe responds by saying; give it to this one, he/she will appreciate and value it!

It's Time... to cultivate an attitude of gratitude... and watch what unfolds in the drama of the universe!

Stop the Traffic

The number of misunderstandings, mishaps and conflicts that take place as a result of the heavy traffic of wasteful and negative thoughts is astounding. For example: a simple situation takes place and each party uses their imagination, constructs their own interpretation, and then reads volumes into it. They then spice it up a bit more and add some spin. The result: a straightforward situation has now become a complicated saga! Over thinking has become an epidemic of our times. We make molehills not only into mountains, but also into overheated volcanoes! Anything small can become a cause for a major outrage. With our minds working on overdrive everything becomes a big deal and we begin to ask why, what, how? Sometimes we can be so preoccupied with details that they take over the whole show. We can become suspicious, doubting, irate or offended. We worry, agonise, fear and fret.

How much surplus thought do we give to an event, even before and after it takes place? Does everything need to be exaggerated and embellished with our thought energy? Can things not be kept simple, uncomplicated, with fewer and finer thoughts? Or is it that we are just too habituated to the idea of overspending in every area including the capital of our thoughts. Why are we wasting our precious energy needlessly?

As we give way to our imagination, the possibilities are endless. We can almost drown in a quagmire of waste and negative thoughts. When the mind is too active, it is harder to control. Very much like a car at high speed, it's hard to stop, and we can easily get into a spin. Learning to not think too much will do more for our health than anything else. Slowing down our thoughts, thinking fewer, more calming thoughts, will give more life to our cells.

Try not to read too much into situations, making them bigger than they are. Everything is what it is – accept it. For example, if someone didn't come to your party when they promised they would, then don't be surprised or raise the question as to why they didn't come, or speculate that they don't like you, etc. How you perceive events is all in your head. You can analyse all you want, but in the end you are just wasting your time and giving yourself sorrow. Be kind to yourself instead by staying positive and in your self-respect.

By over-thinking, we can certainly make the story sound more colourful and juicy, but the problem is that time will only reveal a bitter ending! We will realise that all of our thinking about the other person or event was just our imagination at work, and it was our crooked thinking that made it look so bad! By then it's too late and we may well have lost good friendship.

On the other hand we can also become our own worst enemy, when it comes to making positive changes. By over thinking, we can easily lose momentum. Once you have the thought, just do it! Get on with it. The more you delay as you think about whether you should do it or not, the more the motivating force will dwindle away.

Raja Yoga Meditation teaches us we can't literally stop our thoughts. However, we can certainly practise slowing them down and pausing them, just as one has to stop at the red traffic lights. In the same way, plan for yourself a daily timetable in which you stop for a few minutes every now and then to check the traffic of your thoughts! How fast are your thoughts racing? And are you in control, or is the situation in front of you controlling you?

It's Time... to stop the traffic of your thoughts. Accept them. Go with the flow. Don't give yourself sorrow by over thinking. Be kind to yourself, and create a sweet happy ending to the story!

How Common is Common Sense

Common sense is something all of us are endowed with, yet it often seems to be in short supply. As the pace of the world speeds up, it seems that common sense is becoming increasingly uncommon, and many of us are guilty of not applying it at times when it is most needed.

Common sense is an instinctive, appropriate response to every day events that helps make life simpler and smoother. In order to have common sense one does not need to have specialised knowledge or be super intelligent; it's simply an innate understanding of how to behave, what to do, when and how to do it, and doing it in the right place and time. It's a natural and automatic response to a situation, not something that needs to be deliberated over.

Take things on a personal level: How many times do you find yourself not applying common sense and doing clumsy things like picking up a hot pan without using oven mitts, or speeding when road signs state, for a very good reason, that you should be driving at 30 or 40. Or, lighting a cigarette, which you have just taken from a packet that tells you clearly that it is killing you! Dropping a banana skin on the pavement is not good common sense: picking it up before someone slips on it, is!

Where is our awareness when we make these common-but-sensless choices? We condemn the hot pan on the stove, or the child on the street at the time of speeding, but seldom take responsibility for our own actions. It's not so much a sign of losing our mind; it is misusing our mind, and not being in control of our thoughts. The reasons may be carelessness, laziness, lack of attention, to name just a few. But the real root cause is a lack of awareness. We need to work mindfully and not mindlessly.

Not only that, but the world seems to be losing collective common sense. For example, as people were recently meeting in the world climate change conference COP19 in Warsaw, scientists in New Zealand were discovering proof that the weakening of the earth's crust following a massive earthquake, was due to climate change. Researchers also claim that Typhoon Haiyan which destroyed the Island of Tacloban in the Philippines recently, also happened for the same reasons.

Have we become so selfish and blind to the outcome of our actions, that we are unable to see the cause and effect taking place right in front of our very eyes? How much proof do we need to realise that damaging Mother Earth to this extent is like committing suicide. Do we realise that our future depends on the choices we make at every moment?

The reason that we don't have access to our own common sense is because we are so preoccupied with people and events – who said what to whom, what happened and why, thoughts of doubt and confusion, regrets of the past and worries about the future – that we forget to live in the present moment. We are always somewhere else with our mind.

In order to tap into my own inner wisdom am I aware? Am I living in the present moment and ready to respond to the next moment with calmness and composure, or is my mind in a thousand different places?

What is needed here is spiritual intelligence. If I become internally quiet then I can access my inner wisdom. Common sense is common because we all have it; we just need to reconnect with it.

It's Time… to be aware of the moment and to apply common sense to our daily lives. As the turmoil in the world increases, let us be mindful and not mindless and emerge our innate spiritual wisdom. Live in the moment and you will know exactly what to do when.

Awaken Your Inner Power and Potential

As the world becomes an increasingly challenging place to live in we need to find new insights and new tools to manage ourselves within it. We need to reclaim control as the directors and stewards of our own lives.

The golden age of technology that we are currently passing through has placed at our finger tips the opportunity to access information from anywhere and at any time. We can find out how to assemble a car, predict stormy weather and find a recipe to bake a cake; learn about amoebas and genetics and even track people through GSM-GPS devices. In fact, there is even a 'do it yourself' guide to human enlightenment! We have all the necessary technology for efficient and effective communication and yet one of the biggest problems facing relationships is the communication breakdown.

During the Renaissance, individuals encumbered by medieval philosophy were left behind. Now in the Information and Communication Age, 'medieval' thinkers are threatened with extinction! Now is the time to move into a new paradigm, from information to knowledge, and further, into the realm of personal experience.

When we are caught up in a web of information and activity overload, we cannot find our personal truth, or the time to live it. We have lost sight of our inner power as we strive for the material and the intellectual.

What is inner power and how do we reconnect with it and develop it? How do we identify and uncover hidden potential? What is our inner power and potential asking of us at this time?

In fact, inner power can be identified as many things:

Firstly it is an inner calm where nothing and no one can shake my personal dignity. A strong resolve where one is firm and assured in their virtues i.e. they know there is no other way than virtue. The strength to not lose one's cool and control in the face of difficulty and challenge – no matter what! The power to let go, transcend and move on. The power to stay dispassionate and focused.

Perhaps, the greatest definition of power would be the ability to do what you want when you want – a complete sense of freedom as well as competency. This principle applies to both external and internal power. There is no point having a Ferrari that can speed up to 200km/hr and not having the ability to step on the brake pedal when needed.

Our greatest treasure is our thoughts and inner power is generated by creating pure, positive, peaceful, powerful and purposeful thoughts – the 5 P's! If we allow our mind to wander aimlessly then we are reducing our value. Einstein once said, "If I value my time, I become valuable." Likewise, if I value my thoughts, I become valuable.

Memories of past events drain us of our power easily. The future is also no less; it embezzles our energy through fear, worry and doubt. In one day, a million things will arrive, seeking my attention – sucking at my energy that was accumulated arduously and with much dedication. In a power hungry world, different things in life hunt my power. They eat away at my peace, love, happiness and kindness. This is when discernment is so important; knowing where to take my power from and where to give it.

Thus, if I want to become powerful, I have to safeguard the treasure of my thoughts.

It's Time… to observe and enhance the quality of your thoughts. And when you are completely free from negative influences and feel totally in control, then go ahead and press on the gas pedal, for now, you can speed as fast as you want in your 'Ferrari'.

Enough

With inflation knocking on the door, and unemployment statistics rising, people are finding it increasingly difficult to 'keep up with the Jones's'! And yet the urge to buy impulsively and compete with the latest consumer trends, despite not having the bank balance to match it, is ever increasing. Whether it is the acquisition of mobile phones, cars, outfits, perfumes or the latest fashion fads, there is a strong yearning in the soul to 'fit in'. To be like others; to be seen to be affording everything! But where do we draw the line and say it's 'enough'?

How much is enough? If wage earners were questioned as to whether they found their salaries to be satisfactory, it would be interesting to know the answers. Do most people not feel they should be earning more? And if so, how much more is it going to take to gratify the soul?

How many pairs of shoes are enough? How many clothes do we need in our wardrobe to dress us? How much food in our pantry is enough to feed us? How do we gauge this balance between need and greed? In fact everything can be enough when the heart is big and generous and when it's not, then nothing is enough.

Waste is a relative term. What is waste to one may be a necessity to another! Someone may sit for four hours in meditation a day as they feel it an absolute need in the soul, others may consider this an absolute waste of time. Someone may spend two hours daily in the gym and others may consider this a waste of time. Someone may take a whole plateful and another may judge that as gluttony. Therefore it is important not to judge another for what their 'needs' maybe. Suffice it to say, one needs to look within, at themselves, and check where they are wasting their time, money and other resources. What is the excess in my life that I can trim or put to a better use?

Whether one earns 10 in their currency or 10,000, the body can only create the same appetite. So why take on the added stress? Be happy with the little you have because with that little, you may have a lot more peace, autonomy, independence and many other freedoms that money cannot buy. Sometimes there is a deep hunger to over work and stretch the mile to prove oneself; to compete, to be something or somebody in the world. Though would you not say this sort of proving is primarily to ones self! And if that is the case, is it necessary for the soul to prove anything to itself?

There is a place for ambition and goal setting, but not when it butchers my peace and sanity. The restlessness, agitation and impatience created by desire means the end result will be of a similar nature. If I can't be happy with a little, I will never be happy with a lot!

In order to cultivate contentment, one needs to reassure the self that the original nature of the soul is in fact that of abundance. One has mistaken this to mean acquisition of people and possessions on a more external level. Although having said that, the feeling of abundance in the soul does indeed attract external wealth but by then the soul has moved onto other heights of happiness.

It is because of a deep knowledge of having everything 'once upon a time' that the soul strives for more of the same feeling. This is the reason why any form of lack in one's life is intolerable and throws one into victim mode. But to get oneself out of this pit, one needs to cultivate contentment on a conscious level. I literally need to tell myself that I have enough of everything that I need in this moment. As Mahatma Gandhi once said: there is enough for everyone's need but not everyone's greed.

The sense of lack in the soul is due to an equally deep lack of self worth. It is only when I realise that I deserve better that I will put an end to abuse and ill-treatment. That is when I need to put my foot down and say enough is enough. And in that moment I am not speaking to the other party, I am speaking to myself for having given my power away for so long to too many people and it's enough.

There is also another side to 'enough'. There is a calm and tranquillity when I have given enough time to planning and preparation. If I am scurrying to the airport at the last minute there is going to be stress and strain, which could have easily been avoided, had I left enough time and prepared for the journey.

It's Time… to appreciate all in one's life and to say to the Universe that I do indeed have enough. This will not stop me from aspiring to become a better person as I know I have not quite had enough of the peace and happiness! And as I plan and prepare in life, I can be at peace knowing that I have enough time to get to my destination.

The Art of Asserting Yourself

It's Friday. Your boss has a habit of giving you urgent work at the last minute. As a consequence you have to stay late almost every night to finish it – in fact you have been working late all this week. Today is your partner's birthday and you wish to spend the evening with him or her. You need to leave on time tonight. It's 4:30 p.m. and suddenly your boss appears with an urgent document that needs to be finished by tomorrow morning. How do you deal with the request?

Learning to be assertive at home or at work is definitely a skill we can all use to help us get the most mileage out of life and that is happiness. It should not be confused with aggressive behaviour, which mostly arises from a place of low self worth and feelings of competition and jealousy. By using aggressive behaviour we may get what we want, but it will come at a huge price, perhaps even at the cost of sacrificing a relationship.

Assertiveness is defined as a skill that helps us to communicate our needs and feelings clearly and confidently to others without hurting them. Assertiveness is defined as an attitude of mind. It lets others know that we value ourself, our time, other people and resources. Assertiveness is a behaviour that respects both the self and other people.

People who find it difficult to assert themselves are usually people who are not so happy with themselves and their lot in life! Mildly put, they don't see the point of asserting themselves. They feel undeserving with no sense of self-worth, the inner voice is just not able to speak loud enough. And if this sentence speaks to you, rest assured, you are not alone!

Our level of self-esteem and self-worth will definitely determine how much we stand up for ourselves, voice our opinion and let others know how we would like to be treated. There is a saying in the theatre that there are no small parts, only small actors. So if you feel your part is too small, you are the one who can change that.

A lack of assertiveness is a major cause of feelings of uneasiness and discomfort that millions of people experience. Learning to assert ourselves can help us build confidence and claim our rights in a way that is peaceful and harmonious. Assertiveness is where we can state our point of view in a way that does not upset other people. This is because we are coming from a place of balance. If we don't make this effort, we find ourselves suffering from either an inferiority or superiority complex. Some of the tell tale signs of this are depression, feeling stifled, upset, exploited and many more. Yet sadly, no one is doing this to us. When we lack assertive skills, we are giving people permission to take advantage of us.

There is a difference between passive, assertive and aggressive behaviour. In passive behaviour, the person will express his or her needs, wants, opinions, feelings, beliefs in an apologetic way. While the assertive person will express them in a direct and honest way. The aggressive person will act inappropriately; being rude and disrespectful. Those with passive behaviour do not stand up for their own rights and needs and in doing so puts the rights and needs of others before their own. In assertive behaviour people stand up for themselves in a way that respects other people. With aggressive behaviour, these people stand up for their own rights, but do so in a way that shows disrespect and disregard for the rights of others.

To practice assertive behaviour it helps to know some of our rights in the journey of life. Once we recognise these, they increase our confidence to stand up for what we believe without feeling apologetic.

You have the right to:

- Be different and unique
- Ask for what you want
- Make mistakes
- Admit that you don't know or don't understand
- Say no
- Be heard
- Be treated with respect
- Hold and express different views and opinions from those of other people
- Change your mind
- Privacy

It can be very challenging to begin to change the habits of a lifetime... but if we have the will to change then we can gain the skills to change. There are many books courses out there which can help with the theory. But I believe that the power to transform from a place of low self-esteem to a sense of real self-worth can only come through practicing deep self-appreciation and meditation. Raja Yoga tells us that in essence we are powerful beings, and all of the resources we require to make this shift are within us already. We just need to use them.

And when we reach to that place… then we can be polite yet resolute with the boss. We are more able to state our case. We can negotiate or give our reasons without feeling guilty. We will respect ourselves and the other party, and will probably be a lot better respected for doing so. In short, an attitude of assertiveness can create a better outcome for all.

It's Time… to increase your self-esteem and to practice the art of being assertive. Know that you have a right to say no. Respect yourself and then the vibration and tone that will arise will be one of respect and regard for others.

iCrazy

The high definition screen of social cyberspace paints a very different picture to the one we live out in 'real' life - one with piles of happy photographs, thousands of 'friends', several 'like' clicks and heaps of fans. But behind the promise of an idealised existence where we can be whatever we want to be with unlimited power at our fingertips, the hard facts offer a different and sad story.

Research has indicated that the utopian Internet is in fact making people crazier, lonelier, nauseous, depressed, anxious, impolite, dumber, antisocial and more prone to becoming obsessive and compulsive as well as suffering from Attention Deficit Disorder (ADD).

Have we ever stopped to wonder what will happen when the plug is pulled and we are left without any connectivity... the day we have to finally face ourselves?

Peter Whybrow, the director of the Semel Institute for Neuroscience and Human Behavior at UCLA, argues that "the computer is like electronic cocaine," fuelling cycles of mania followed by depressive stretches. It "fosters our obsessions, dependence, and stress reactions," adds Larry Rosen, a California psychologist who has researched the Net's effect for decades. It "encourages—and even promotes—insanity." (Newsweek-The Daily Beast, by Tony Dokoupil)

The engine of social media and instant communication is now so ingrained in many people's psyche that it is impossible to switch it off. It is rewiring us, forming a new breed of unhealthy relationships and fantasies, where we are losing control of ourselves. It has a hold on us that we may dislike but one we cannot resist. People get on the Net even before getting out of bed expecting to catch the next ping, ring or ding!

If this obsession continues, it is likely our next generation will grow up with a smartphone in hand, face down and completely devoid of human contact and interpersonal skills – in a word – a zombie!

If you think you are immune to this disease, then just check the number of times you check your cell phone or emails in one day. What would happen to you physically and emotionally if this electronic cocaine were to be taken away for even a day?

The conclusion of an experiment 'unplugged' conducted by the University of Maryland in 2010 asking 200 undergrads to forgo all Web and mobile technologies for a day and to keep a diary of their feelings was "most college students are not just unwilling, but functionally unable to be without their media links to the world".

The term Internet is a misnomer, instead of taking us inward into ourselves, it should be termed 'outernet', taking us to the farthest corners of reality, and very far away from our inner core, our true being.

Before we get too lost in cyberspace with our Gravatars, it's time to remember that we are human "beings". Perhaps it's time to get back to basics and re-build some real relationships - first of all with ourselves, and then with the people sitting in the same room, completely free from the reliance of any electrical wire!

From the invention of electricity, to motorcars, to instant connectivity – technology has some great things to offer and our lives would be much less comfortable without it. However it is time to reclaim our own inner power and to remember just who should be in the driver's seat. Who is the master? Me or the machine? I or the iPad?

We need also to remember that when the battery of the soul is down, nothing in our lives will work. It is essential to recharge and refresh regularly for inner power and optimum results. The only place to refill that power is with God, the Divine. No amount of 'outernet' activity can replenish the soul, on the contrary it will only deplete it. The wireless communication we are truly seeking is the one with God, the one who is constantly charged and overflowing with the spark of excitement the soul really seeks.

It's Time… to face the real people in the real world and go back to basics. Spend a day or even half a day away from the Net or your mobile phone to enjoy your own company. Then when you finally get tired of your virtual reality there's a real one just a thought away...

No Complaints

Have you ever heard of the expression, 'the squeaky wheel gets oiled?' 'Squeakers', or in other words, complainers, often get attended to because no one wants to listen to their constant whining. They make the loudest noise and therefore achieve results, but at what cost? Continuous whining or squeaking does not win friends.

Today's world is full of complainers. Some are justifiably seeking the resolution of an injustice, some are genuinely trying to make things better, but some just like to complain!

At the heart of a complaint is a grievance of some kind or another. Perhaps the shop sold us some faulty goods. Perhaps a work colleague is trying to bully us. These types of complaints will actually bear more fruit if we make them dispassionately, when the heat of the emotion has cooled down. It is also prudent to direct the complaint at the right person, rather than broadcasting it for anyone who wants to hear. This approach takes self-respect and a certain amount of detachment, but a cool head, rather than a heart filled with fury, is certainly the more effective approach.

Some people seem to make complaining a hobby. The dissatisfaction in this case stems from within; when we don't feel good inside we project this into the outside world, and onto others. If I am not happy with myself then I will never be happy with what's going on around me. So check: am I a complainer? If so, it is a good indication that I have some more inner work to do. When I feel good from inside, then the 'reason' for most of my complaints may just magically disappear! Then people will find me much more pleasant to be around.

It's no surprise that we are put off by complaints; on the surface they don't sound very constructive and when directed at us can make us feel annoyed, angry, resentful or hopeless. We don't often receive them well. We strive day and night to make our world picture perfect but don't always succeed, so when others complain about us, or the way we do things, we can feel resentful, inadequate or insecure.

Handling complaints from others is an art, and rather than trying to deflect them, or reject them, we may do better to reflect on them. When someone is complaining it is usually because they feel that their vision of the end result is better than ours, or they feel the need to correct us because they feel we have strayed from our own vision. In the heat of the moment when words are spoken passionately, the focus on the vision or the end result unfortunately gets lost. We tend to project most of our energy in protecting ourselves, rather than trying to understand the real reason for it. "Well, it's not my fault. I have done all that I can, what more can I do?" We can often take it personally; we shrivel up inside, and wonder: "What's the point?"

We don't recognise that, if we could only step back from our emotional response for a moment, we could perhaps gain an understanding of what the complainer is really reflecting back to us.

Firstly, stay calm. It may not be personal; it may just be someone channeling their inner frustration on the person closest to them. Secondly, treat the complainer with respect. Sometimes a complaint is a plea from the heart, the complainer just wants to feel 'heard'. Thirdly, is there any foundation to this complaint? If I have the humility to admit that there is, then this is a good lesson for me, enabling me to address a weakness that I may not have seen in myself before.

It's Time... to complain less and listen more. Try to understand the others point of view as you would like them to understand yours. Realise that the squeaks and groans are an opportunity in disguise, signalling you to compassion and self-respect, and helping you to proactively 'oil' the wheels of your own self-growth.

Anger - One Letter Away From Danger

Anger is a much used but little understood emotion. Many feel justified with their angry reactions and others consider it to be a 'natural' fight or flight response. Yet those who have been down this garden path will realise that anger serves very little purpose and yet creates a lot more damage. It takes away our peace of mind, leaving us weak and empty. There is a lot of information out there about anger management, but on a spiritual path a more relevant question may be how we transform our anger.

Anger – simply a habit

When we do something over and over again it becomes a habit. Anger can be simply a pattern of behaviour that we have created over time as a reaction to a certain situation. Habits by definition are unconscious… so to become conscious and aware of our reactions means that we can step in and use the power of choice. Through responding rather than reacting we can begin to change our destructive thought patterns.

Anger - opposite of peace

The reason we want to be at peace at all times is because peace is our innate and original nature. If we are feeling anything other than that, then we will yearn to return back to that calm and still state. When we feel peace we are able to be in a state of acceptance, and a practiced yogi will realise that, not only is anger a useless emotion, but also that it is unnecessary. When we get angry we are in fact 'out of control' and anger is simply a sign that we are trying to control something that we cannot. This is not wisdom!

If I realise that peace is my personal property, then I can choose whether I want to give it away, or keep it!

Anger – a secondary emotion

Anger is a secondary emotion that surfaces in the form of heated words, a loud tone and wild actions. The primary emotion is ego-based, and springs from fear or a sense of injustice. When the ego feels threatened our knee jerk reaction is to defend the anger.

Anger – a drug

Angry people often don't realise that every time they get angry, the body excretes certain hormones that make them feel good (egotistical!) about themselves. This negative stimulus is like a merciless drug; it gives people a false sense of power. But in reality, it's weak people who feel the need to use anger to manipulate and control others.

Anger – not a stress reliever

People often use the 'anger tool' to release a build up of stress and tension believing it will serve the purpose. However, these angry upsets do little to alleviate stress, if anything, they cause more damage to our health and our relationships. Be aware not to let stress build up. There are many stress-management techniques – Meditation being one of the best!

Anger – lack of discernment

When we are at the peak of our anger, we are at the trough of our discrimination and discernment power. In simple words, it make us stupid! This explains why much of the crime in our society is done in the heat of the moment.

If you feel anger coming on count to ten and take a deep breathe.

Anger – a necessary defence

Often people use anger as a means to appear authoritative or to 'get things done'. People are afraid of appearing weak if they don't use anger as their first choice weapon of attack. But the truth is that they may get things done in the short-term, but will not win hearts and minds in the long run. Being assertive, not aggressive, is a much better strategy for success. But to be assertive takes self-respect, and the angry person is usually angry for the very reason that they have low self-esteem.

Anger – is not 'happening' to me

If we chose to see an act of anger against us as simply an act in a drama and nothing more than that, then we would likely not be so affected. Yet we make anger personal. When people use anger against us, just remember that it's THEIR stuff, not yours, and in fact the person they are most angry with is themselves.

It's Time… to change your 'garden path' and to keep away from this danger of anger. While other anger management programs will do just that, manage your anger, meditation will actually heal you of it completely!

Ego Crunch

For centuries psychologists have tried to unearth and understand this elusive, intangible and very complicated subject of the Ego. We all have it, even if we may deny it. We all heavily rely on it to help us get through life. Like actors in a play, we don the costume of our ego and interact with others accordingly, sometimes hardly glimpsing the 'souls behind the roles'.

The ego is our best friend and our worst enemy. We may see it as our valiant defender against the big bad world, we may call it 'self-respect' or 'pride' and yet it causes us a great deal of sorrow. Have you ever felt hurt or insulted by something someone said to you, even (or particularly) if it was true? Of course we all have, and that's the ego at work. Instead of taking this as an opportunity to grow from, the ego defends us, and cuts us off from a valuable life lesson.

Have you ever felt that you have to prove yourself right even at the considerable expense of losing a relationship and living the rest of your life in regret? It's a temptation that can be hard to resist, thanks to the endeavours of the ego.

The ego loves to make us feel superior at one moment, and inferior the next. It likes to indulge in self-pity, self-sabotage and feelings of revenge. It makes us stand up and 'have our say' when it's really more appropriate to sit down and be silent, and it makes us mute, shy and embarrassed the very time that we need to speak up.

In this way we have become a slave to our own egos. Our ego made us think we are always right (or always wrong: inverted ego). It made us believe that we are stronger and intelligent than what we really were, or it made us feel fearful, victimised and aggressive. If we were really to understand that ego is the major cause of wars and bloodshed in the world, then we should stop to ask ourselves, is that super intelligence or sheer stupidity? Who is at war in the world, is it nations, cultures, religions or our egos? Where is the real battlefield, out there or inside our minds?

The ego lied to us. In the false name of pride, we safeguarded it. It was a two-way partnership, a contract of 'you scratch my back and I will scratch yours!' It seized our peaceful inner kingdom, gained supremacy over our mind and thoughts and placed our self-respect behind bars.

We may justify that we had to create this unreal identity in order to find our way in a sometimes-hostile world, but we paid a huge price – pain in direct proportion to its size.

For a spiritual seeker it is important to bid farewell to the ego. The ego is the greatest, if not the only, barrier to self-realisation and eternal permanent happiness. We shall all one day have to crush it to arrive at our real and higher self. If we do not do this work ourselves, then we will die a thousand deaths before the ego is finally laid to rest.

The ego crunch, not to be confused with the Nestle chocolate Crunch, is not such a sweet experience. The ego has been our companion for a long time, it will put up a real fight and the process can be painful, unpleasant, uncomfortable and harrowing, but the end result is fulfilling and rewarding. It is an awakening, an illumination, a liberation. The fog of our skewed and distorted thinking begins to clear and the feeling is of having finally awoken out of the clutches of a deep sleep of ignorance.

To crunch the ego we have to be prepared to be 'wrong', to look foolish, small and passive, and we have to let go of judgement, blame, criticism and false pride. When the ego dies, it takes along its many relatives.... fear, hatred, anger, selfishness, and a whole progeny that had hijacked our happiness all along. It is not a small thing to become egoless, and it is not for the faint-hearted. However, the rewards are boundless.

The ego will have to die eventually anyway, and crunching it before it's crunched for us is a wise thing to do. There is a simple yardstick that we can use to help us. If it hurts, it's ego! Because if there is no ego, there is no threat and nothing to defend!

It's Time... to crunch the EGO before it crunches us!

The Art of Driving

If you have ever learned to drive you will know that it takes time, effort and often many mistakes, before we become really proficient.

You may also have noticed that life is a bit like that. One difference is that in life we are not given a manual to follow, rather we learn by experience. Also we take not just one, but many tests along the way.

As in driving, life may seem to us like a challenging journey, fraught with obstacles and danger. Some may take little delight in it, seeing it as a tedious chore to be endured. However when we feel that we are fully in the driving seat of life, confident and in control, then it becomes fun, interesting, exhilarating and an adventure. Both the journey and the destination are important and knowing that we are 'on the right road' we can enjoy every moment of the ride.

Of course there are some basics that we can't leave home without, for example we need to know how to control our vehicle, we need to know where we are going, and it's useful to have a map, a compass (or the latter–day equivalent, a sat nav) and it's also important to know the rules of the road.

When I (the soul) am in charge of my vehicle (the body) the same applies. On my journey of life it's always advisable to have a destination in mind. When we are clear about where we want to get to, we can select the best and most appropriate route. Then, even if we stop off to admire the side scenes along the way, we won't get lost, or forget where we're heading.

The 'rules of the road' are our spiritual values and principles, these are our internal indicators which guide and protect us and which, when followed, will allow us to negotiate the roadwork's, potholes and other obstacles en route, ensuring that we get to our destination happily and safely.

And, of course we are not the only ones on a journey. What about all of the other drivers on the road? Do we sometimes lose control of ourselves, crash around and bump into them, while at the same time blaming them for their bad driving? Or do we engage our intellect, move ahead calmly and purposefully, and know exactly when to accelerate, when to manoeuvre, and when to apply the brakes?

It's Time… to drive our lives safely and calmly. We all drive on the same roads, and are given the same set of rules. How enjoyable, interesting, exciting or productive my journey turns out to be, is entirely up to me. It's interesting to note how, when we're feeling well tuned and on top of the world, all the traffic lights seem to be on green for us and we coast towards our destination. However, if we encounter too many red lights, roadblocks or irate drivers on the journey, maybe that's a signal that, even though the vehicle might be in reasonable condition, the driver may need to take a few more lessons.

The School of Hard Knocks

There are two types of people in the world: the pessimists and the optimists. The optimist sees every challenging situation as an opportunity to grow while the pessimist views the same situation as doom and disaster. Life presents us with a variety of knocks and bangs in the form of situations and experiences and it's totally up to us how we deal with them. Those who grab the opportunity to change, move forward, grow and excel whilst those who fear and become intimidated, lose out, stay stuck and miss the valuables lessons that life brings! Which personality are you?

It would do us well to view life as a perpetual school, in which every soul and situation is enabling us to attain our 'Masters Degree' in life! Everyone and everything are our teachers and we are being refined by every challenge and opportunity.

It's as though we are pieces of rock and life is sculpting and shaping us. We are being chipped at and chiselled to perfection. Life will continue to attempt to knock us over, unbalance us and make us loose our footing. We may lose our job, a close friend or partner, or have an accident. But those who accept the lessons, pick themselves up and become wiser for it, can make their lives a masterpiece.

For every piece of art to be created, the artist needs silence and concentration. A painter, a sculptor, an architect, each need solitude and quiet to get their work done. If we take time to stand back, observe, reflect, and use our inner wisdom, we will learn that everything that is happening to us is exactly as it should be. We will be totally grateful for the tests that life is presenting to us and thankful for the work of art we are becoming!

You will have noticed that you do not respond to the same situation now as you would have done in your teens or twenties – the reason being that life has shaped you and you will be more experienced, wiser and more mature. With time, introverts become extroverts, extroverts become introverts, those seeking the limelight will look out for the 'dimlight', those who exercised anger and ego will be humbled with patience… but this depth of transformation will only apply to those who actually take the time to use the lessons of life to their advantage. For those who resist, for them the hard knocks will persist.

Choose to always keep a positive frame of mind no matter what. Things may look pretty bad, but in hindsight we often realise how perfect they were for our growth. The art and the power is to be able to remember all this when we are passing through the situation and not after it.

It's Time… to see everything that happens to you in life as an opportunity for your growth and learning. Don't resist it accept it. Realise that every lesson is tailor-made for your greater good. Be grateful that the lesson has come, it has come to you and it has come now and not in your old age. Don't wait until it's too late!

Dancing with Your Inner Dragon

According to the Chinese calendar, the Oriental Dragon is regarded as a divine beast. It is said to be a symbol of good fortune and a bringer of health and wealth.

As we move into the year of the Dragon (23rd January, the 4709th year according to Chinese mythology) Chinese communities and many others around the world will be celebrating - and the dancing red dragon will make its appearance as the main feature of the carnival parades.

The Chinese Dragon is much revered as a wise protector, noble and powerful. It is the imperial symbol, an image of vitality, power and wealth.

Yet this mythical creature when it appears in western stories is a fearsome, terrifying beast that needs to be either pacified (by feeding it a sacrifice) or by conquering or killing it. The dragon of these fables is sometimes seen as a symbol for Satan.

The Patron Saint of England, Saint George, another mythical figure, who is invariably depicted on his horse wielding his sword in the act of slaying the dragon.

In fact this myth is thought to have emerged from the ancient Middle East, with its roots going back even further to Greek legend. Saint George, so the story goes, heroically rescued a princess in distress who was about to be devoured by the dragon, and also saved a whole town from the terror of the monster that no-one else could overcome.

It is interesting to note that the same beast (which never actually existed in the real world as far as we know) should have two very opposing sets of attributes.

Could it be that this imaginary beast, at its worst, reflects what is in each of us? Do we not each have a fire-breathing dragon within, lurking in the shadows, ready to pounce (and punch) at any moment? Is not the human ego capable of producing the same destructive results as a dragon on a rampage? Perhaps the malevolent, evil and hateful elements of human nature have been given a shape, name and form so that we can 'demonise' these attributes without having to admit that they are in fact a part of us!

Lust, anger, violence, greed, attachment and ego are very definitely characteristics of human nature today, but are they really part of our original 'true' nature? Do we secretly enjoy our inner dragon, and let it loose, breathing fire on unsuspecting others, just to show them who's boss and who's in control? Does it sometimes emerge from us when we are not expecting it, or even when we don't want it to? Our inner dragon certainly seems to have a mind of its own!

It's not easy coming to terms with our inner ferocious self. Mostly the dragon of the fables shows its head when its need is not met, like food or water. Likewise, we can become irritable, angry and even cruel when we have not fed ourselves the diet of good, positive, peaceful and fulfilling thoughts. Because if we continue to keep this dragon well fed on a diet of criticism, judgement and blame then the stronger and more piercing the fire that will emerge from our mouth and our eyes, the damage which we will often later regret.

St George killed the dragon by piercing it under its wing, where there were no hard scales to protect it. Likewise, it's only when we let down our own ego-defences that we have a chance to kill the inner dragon. Although others may try and 'kill' or 'tame' that ego of ours, yet this genuine inner work is something only I can do for myself. And when that moment comes, it is a triumph - no fear, only freedom. We will then have the dragon follow like a meek beast on our leash of victory.

Continue to focus on your gentler and noble self – stop the masquerade. Better than fighting the devil within, is to emerge the magnificent, wise, confident, strong and free-spirited dragon. After all, it is the dragon that you choose to feed that will grow stronger. Like the dancing dragon in the street, be spiritually attractive, flamboyant and one full of life and joy - this aspect of the dragon is also within us. People will not fear you because of your uncontrollable vices, but instead respect you for the command of your virtues.

It's Time... to be strong, courageous and to slay the negative dragon within, that ruthless, demanding, egocentric, defensive, power-mad, foolhardy and pompous inner self and to emerge that dancing spirit, vibrant, magnanimous, charismatic, principled, noble-hearted, healthy and shrewd. Then you can really celebrate!

Calm and Confident

Are You the Captain of Your Ship?

In these turbulent times, with the winds of change blowing at an ever increasing speed, there is a greater need than ever before to take charge of our ship of life and navigate it to calmer shores.

At times we may be heading in the 'right' direction, yet other forces may rock the boat. At such times, we are called upon to use the experiences we have gained thus far and patiently ride out the storm. A difficulty only encourages us to be more attentive in life, just as a strong wind alerts the captain of a probable storm.

To be the captain means to take charge of your ship – to have the spiritual, mental, and emotional skills to navigate your life; to forecast the weather and decide which crew to have on board.

When caught in a storm, the captain's first and foremost duty is the safety of his passengers. He then looks at his compass and determines north. An experienced captain will steer the ship to the centre of the storm, not try to run from it; for that is the safest place. Once in the centre, the ship travels with the storm until it subsides.

On any given day, on the same wind, one ship may sail east while another west. The position of their sails determines their direction and not the direction of the wind. Hence, we cannot blame the winds of change for the direction in which we are headed. We need to position our sails in the direction we would like to see our life heading.

Storm or no storm, while navigating the sea of life, we need to get out our compass from time to time, and find our true north. Our north is our purpose, the reason why we are here on Mother Earth. For some it's to share and communicate and yet for others it's to continually cause grief and sorrow!

Our compass is made up of our personal values and principles – in which direction are these pointing? If they are not aligned to our north, our purpose, then there is a lack of congruence between our thoughts and actions i.e. the direction we need to be heading in. For example, if my life purpose is to communicate or share information, then my vocation needs to be in the area of sharing wisdom and information, such as training, writing or public speaking. If instead, I am stuck in a job like event management or manual work then my spirit is not going to be fulfilled.

And it is this discrepancy that blows in the gales and hurricanes of discontent and restlessness in the mind. I am forever seeking something, but not quite knowing how to get there. If you feel that you are aboard a ship other than yours then it is time for you to stop for a moment, check your inner compass and ask yourself who or what is navigating your life.

Take charge of your life! You and only you are at the helm. Only you can determine your state of happiness or the status of your inner peace, or the quality of your contentment.

It's Time… to take a good look at your horizon, watch the winds, re-position your sails and sail forth!

To Push or to Pull?

How often do we find ourselves pushing for certain things in life when with a little shift in attitude, a twist of consciousness and a swing in the right direction we can actually, 'pull' or attract the things we need quite easily.

Learning to recognise the things we need to push away or pull towards us in our life, takes time, attention and focus. In fact, normally we push where we need to pull and pull where we need to push. When dieting for example, we push away certain foods from the body, instead of pulling the right foods towards us that will help to eliminate the toxins and fats. Or, in our neediness we push to make a relationship work, which results only in us pushing away the other person, rather than pulling them towards us with genuine love and a little extra care and patience.

If you find yourself pushing too hard to achieve things in life it means you are definitely not in the flow of the drama. In fact you are paddling against the current, which can be very taxing on the mind and body. This does not mean however, that you should not persist or persevere. Knowing just when to hold on to something and when to let it go is an art that comes with time and experience.

When the consumer markets are pushing too many products at us, it's important to be able to discriminate between the want and the need.

Their pushing their wares onto us, does not mean that we need to pull them towards us! Learn to discern clearly and you will discover that there is very little you have to pull towards you; with the right intention, whatever you need will come in front of you.

Very often harried parents will use the strategy of pushing things away from their children such as: "don't do this", "don't do that", "don't sit there", etc. If the pull strategy was employed instead, the parent would lovingly encourage, build confidence and help the child to develop a strong sense of self-respect. In this way the parent will gain respect and authority and the child will learn for him or herself to make better choices.

And when it comes to the subject of spirituality, instead of grappling to push away the aspects of ourselves that we don't like, it's much more effective to pull towards yourself the truth of who you are: Love, Light, Peace and Joy. When we focus on the negativity within us we then give it even more energy and it takes an even greater hold over us. When we switch on the light and self-realise our inner beauty, power, and potential, then the darkness will evaporate.

It's Time… to stop pushing and to draw towards you the things you really need in life. What you resist persists therefore let go of the struggle… and invite abundance into your life.

Balanced Spirit

It's easy to see that many of us are living out of balance. When we are not in balance, we feel it, hear it, and sense it. Our return to balance can only truly occur when we place the needs of the soul on a par with our physical needs. We have moved our focus away from the pearl, the inner self, to the shell, the outer self.

From our deepest core we are interconnected – souls living in a balanced cyclic wisdom that has existed since eternity. Circadian rhythms govern our waking and sleeping, our time for activity and rest, hunger and repleteness. Thus our yearning for balance is completely natural, for our soul and body seek only to live in harmony with the rhythm of the natural world around us, that is, in complete balance.

To everything there is a season; nature has the natural wisdom to balance itself if left alone, however we have consciously and unconsciously intervened, losing not only our own balance but upsetting the balance of the universe in the process.

We can observe harmony in the mandala and magic circles of the indigenous people; in the Chinese yin and yang; in the eight-fold path of the Buddha; the Hindus have the wheel of life, Islam depicts harmony in the crescent moon and star and Christianity the balanced cross.

Our habit is usually to pay attention to the sound and not enough to the silence, as if it is unnatural to do so; we fill up the gaps of calm with deafening music, dull conversations or the loud TV. However, it is only a matter of time before everything begins to change and although out of confusion and uncertainty we may vacillate for some time, we eventually are forced to adapt, juggle, harmonise and balance! For every sound arises out of silence and buries itself in silence. We were born out of silence and will merge into the silence.

We cannot remain in any extreme state for too long, we have to find our centre. In fact, we learn more about living in balance when we are out of balance. The first step is awareness and the second is acceptance. This juggling act of trying to find our balance is a life long lesson. In the serenity prayer, we ask God to help us accept the things we cannot change and the strength to change the things we can. This embodies our daily struggle as well as reminds us of how to succeed and be agents of positive change.

Balance is very important; it is about walking the tightrope of life on all levels: emotional, spiritual and physical, not simply being able to manage my daily timetable. One needs enough discipline and attention, and yet ease and a nature that is simple and flowing. Too much stiffness and one can fall, and not enough makes the crossing even more dangerous.

There is no motion without stillness and no stillness without motion. Emotion is known as energy in motion. And so instead of riding the roller coaster of emotions, sit still, centre yourself inside and harness the energy within and you will feel a profound sense of peace, power and balance.

With the practice of meditation we re-learn how to harmonise with the world around us. In fact, the beauty of meditation is to be able to feel the stillness amidst the chaos and touch the silence surrounded by sound, to begin to see light where we previously only saw darkness and to give love where anger once prevailed.

It's Time… to realise that spirituality is full of paradoxes; therefore let go, start your journey of acceptance and you will feel in control. Be productive in service and you will find your peace. Check your comfort and 'uncomfort' zones to find what you can relieve and grow from. Finding balance is also like learning to ride a bicycle… at times you may topple… until the balance becomes completely natural!

Expression and Experience

The purpose of life can be summed up in two words: Expression and Experience. Everything we do, we do to express a particular quality from within the soul and at the same time we continue to experience various qualities of the Universe through people and nature.

This is perhaps more obvious when we take time out to go on holidays. When our sole purpose is to just sit… relax… and… soak in the sights and sounds from our chosen travel destination. As our time there is limited and we are exposed to new cultures and ways, we may take the courage to try out new things too — adding to our bank of experiences.

The very nature of the soul is to express – it is like breath, life, for the soul. In fact, this is the reason the soul enters and inhabits a body. Without a body the soul cannot 'feel'. As the soul communicates through a body, it is illustrating the qualities of the soul. The output of which can only be what has been the input! Thus, we often comment that the face is the mirror or the index of the mind, or that our actions speak volumes (of the mind!).

The soul can be likened to a puppeteer and the body its puppet. How the puppeteer handles the puppet will depend on his/her puppet management skills! In the same vein, the soul is known as the raja, the king, and the body – with its five senses of sensation and perception -its kingdom. How well do I the king manage my kingdom on a daily basis? Or do the senses manage me: telling me to eat another slice of the cream cake, or to listen to the gossip a little while longer, or to continue watching the horror movie, knowing too well that it will hound me in my dreams later!

There is no machine as sophisticated and complex as the human body and no operator as ingenious as the soul. The soul is the spark, the fuel, the energy, which ignites the body. Without this light the body is a corpse. Since all the essential organs are intact — the brain, the heart etc. — this could only mean one thing and that is... the life force, the breath has left, gone, finito, khalas!

Some senses execute certain thoughts whilst others absorb thoughts tossed over by the universe (and some do both!). For example, the eyes can give a look that can kill or a look that sparks a romance. If the eyes are erased in someone's picture, it's hard to even identify the person. The eyes are the windows to the world. Without sight we lose one fifth of our connection with the world. In the same way, the mouth can give hope to someone through a few kind words, or it can destroy relationships for a lifetime! Noses normally want something "fragrant" or pleasant to smell or else we 'turn up our noses'! And the sense of touch should be all about love and care, not abuse and cruelty.

So since we know our purpose here is to express and experience, then let us express and experience the highest, the best and most divine. We have the power to choose what we take in and what we emit. The senses simply implement the messages we pass over to them.

As "couch potatoes", we may sit and surface many thoughts such as aspiring to climb Mount Everest; charting a world tour; or trying to conceive brilliant entrepreneurial ideas similar to the likes of Starbucks or Facebook! But it is those who get off the couch and do something that make a difference in the world. Sitting and thinking is not enough, I have to express into action my passion, my power, my zest, my determination, my motivation, my vision and then I am getting closer to achieving my goal.

Just as spring brings out the best in nature, so too there comes a season, a time, when we all need to express, to blossom and bring out our best – we won't be happy or at peace till we have. And just as the dry, barren tree surprises us with tiny, fresh new leaves, so too life surprises us with what we have within us. There is a saying that there is a saint in every sinner and a sinner in every saint. It just depends on whom you feed the most that will grow!

And as we live and experience life and take in like a sponge, let us begin to filter what we absorb. We are not a garbage can that everyone can just throw their stuff into. It's totally up to me which eye glasses to wear and which perspective to take on and which to discard.

It's Time… to get off that couch and do something great today. Express your best and experience the highest that life is offering you. Wear the right eye glasses and you will indeed see that your glass is certainly more than half full. Take charge of your puppet, and if that slice of cake still pulls you, tell it to go and take a hike! After all you are in command – you are the puppeteer!

Take Me to a 'Good Place'

Everything around us is a vibrating energy: the chair you are sitting on, the gadget you are using to view this article, the coffee you have in front of you, the cushion on your back, the photo frame in front of you. And at every single moment there is an exchange of energy between you and everything around you. At every second, you have a choice as to which energies to absorb and which to resist.

The greatest impact is that of other people's energy. If there were a choice, would you rather not work with a polite, kind, modest and easy going person or a bossy, rude, negative and selfish person? What is it about their energies that either attract us or repel us?

The answer is that the former energy will take us to that 'good place' inside of ourselves where our good qualities emerge easily and automatically. The latter takes us to an uncomfortable place filled with fear and insecurity, and where we have to make the effort firstly, to overcome the negative and secondly, to assert our virtue.

Imagine if we had x-ray vision and were able to 'tune' into every one's energy field. Chances are we would certainly keep our distance from many people as we notice the negative quality of their thoughts and feelings.

Every time we shake hands with another individual or come into their proximity, there is an exchange of energy between our auras. We are 'touched' by that person – literally! And our energy fields penetrate each other. No wonder we feel tired and exhausted by the end of the day. Just as we can immediately recognise the energy projected from a holy place of worship or from a night-club, so too we need to be discriminating about places such as shopping malls and sports stadiums.

On the surface they seem to be neutral spaces, but on an energetic level, there is desire, greed, ego, competition and more lurking in the shadows!

Whether we realise it or not, we do become influenced. Sometimes, when we come to our senses we wonder how on earth we could have come to that decision, or bought that particular item, or even why we feel low, unhappy or depressed.

When we see mob violence we see people caught up in this force that will cause them to do things that they would not do otherwise. People will even kill, torture and rape under the persuasive influence of the negative collective energy.

Just as we are selective about the aesthetics of our personal space, it's also important to filter the energies in our life and be selective about the people we hold in our orbit.

We want to be with those who take us to a good place in our minds and hearts, not those who steal our energy or further weaken it with their negativity, or worse, may have bad intentions towards us.

Meditation is an important tool to help us create a very powerful aura of light and purity. In times of need this will be our greatest protection. And the greatest charity we can do for the world will be to spread that light and help raise the vibration of the planet.

It's Time… to notice the energies around you and to tune into the positive. Better still, influence others with your aura of peace, power and love, and help raise the vibration in the world. Take people to that 'good place' inside of themselves.

Be-easy-ness

One of the greatest illusions of our century is that in order to have the space to do what you want to do, you need more time. This need not be so. It is not time that determines the speed of our lives, but we, and the speed of our thoughts. Ten minutes of trauma can feel like several painful hours, and yet 'time flies, when you are enjoying yourself'. Ever thought why?

Because it is thoughts that really take up space, not actions. Think of a time when you procrastinated about completing a job. When you finally got down to doing it, notice how much less time it took than you had imagined earlier. In fact, we work hard to stay busy so that we won't have to face our internal demons or get depressed with our own company! A moment of silence and there is panic. What to do? Who to call? Where to go? In fact, as soon as we get in from work, we scurry to turn on the TV or our favourite music, and we call that 'quiet time'.

Technology too has had a part in this. Having faster modes of communication means we are forced to decide and act faster. In the past it would have taken us a few days or weeks to respond to our love letters and send our responses by ship. This urgency to respond is being thrust upon us now within minutes or hours via text message, email, chat messages etc. What would happen if you did not get an 'I love you' back the very next moment you sent it. You would begin to question your partner's integrity! The value of 24 hours is not the same. And nothing has changed except the speed of our life.

Life is not about becoming a hermit either. "Hands that work are better than lips that pray". In fact the peace that follows action is most restful. The quiet that follows, after resolving someone's unrest is most rewarding.

There is nothing wrong with being busy and active, yet one needs to learn to be easy and flexible at the same time. One needs to create a rhythm; not an empty busy-ness without any melody. Thoughts, speech and actions need to be orchestrated; synchronised. Life has to have a deeper meaning. So which do you work on first, activity or stillness? Well… what value would musical notes have if it were not for the silence in between them? How can you fly when there is no ground to return to? How could you enjoy the days if it were not for those nights of sound sleep?

And what is all the kafuffle for if we are not experiencing sublime peace and bundles of happiness! All the action should have a meaning and purpose behind it; yes we should enjoy the journey, but the destination is equally as important. So if we are to stay busy, then let it be with healthy thoughts, otherwise an 'empty mind is a devil's workshop'! If I have not placed thoughts in my mind, then who has – that is a scary thought! Entertain your mind with clear, peaceful, positive and powerful thoughts.

Between every stimulus and a response, there is a space, a space in which to choose. In that moment, as I choose, I become the master.

Actually when we practice being in a state of soul consciousness which means to be more aware of the soul and its qualities and the experience of the eternity of the soul, then the world slows down for us.

And in mundane or physical consciousness I limit myself; I cannot see beyond what these two eyes reveal to me. There is no internal world to enjoy because I have not developed it. I feel restricted and bound by physical limitations, and that includes time. Furthermore, I convince myself that I am right to think this way just because everyone else does. But the inner voice, the conscience speaks louder.

Practicing soul consciousness for a few minutes every couple of hours will allow you to tune in to the third dimension of life. A frequency that will keep you calm in moments of chaos. And you will find yourself using the expression: 'There is more than what meets the eye'.

It's Time… to take out time in between your busy moments, and to create a silent space in your mind. Keeping the mind light and easy with simple peaceful thoughts, will allow you to savour the moment and complete tasks efficiently. Then you will truly come to know what 'Quiet Time' is!

Have You Got a Minute?

In a world where many of our resources are running out, we seem to forget that time is an equally important asset that is running scarce. We forget that 'life' and 'time' have a connection and that there is only a certain window of opportunity in which to do the things we want to achieve. Our life is precious – we don't have oodles of time nor has science managed to invent a gadget that can create extra time! So how am I using my time, and how can I make the most of it?

Time is just a measurement of an event or experience. Therefore we should really be event managers and not time managers! If we are chasing our tail all the time, then that means we have not mastered time. We are still a slave to the clock. Experiential time is quality time. One in which there is a feeling of order and sense of calm.

Our measure of time has indeed changed over the last 150 years. A single day does not seem to last as long as it did for our forefathers! They used to watch the sun rise… and then set again! Yet with the advent of electricity, we don't even get time to look out the window.

We have to admit there appears to be a time famine. More and more people are finding they have less and less time to do the things they want to do. Could it be due to the increase in ambition and desires or are we fooling ourselves that the day has literally been shortened by something like an Act of God. There is in fact ample time, if we are certain of what we need to be doing.

We spend more time as human 'doings', than as human beings. More and more, people are rushing to get onto their next 'thing' or next 'high'. And in the process, they miss the magic, secret and joy of the moment. In a state of mindfulness, a state of peace, calm and joy, we can enjoy the task at hand and not feel rushed, with still some time and energy for more of the same. We save time this way.

Have you ever wondered why it is that some people achieve so much in a short time, and others so little? Of course there could be a number of factors such as skill and efficiency, but it also has a lot to do with the way they manage their thoughts. Managing thoughts brings clarity. If out of confusion or inner turmoil we create excess thoughts which then need to be sifted, then in the process we may have missed the perfect opportunity and have to start again.

Segregate the urgent vs. important: Putting a report or document together at the office for the auditor may be very urgent, but attending your daughter's graduation maybe more important. Finding meaning and purpose has everything to do with how you prioritise your time and achieve results in relationships. The guilt we create in mis-managing time wears away the will in the soul. Meditation helps us to concentrate, to stay focused on what really matters and as we give that priority we are at peace in our lives.

Gossiping, criticising, idling, dilly dallying, worrying, indolence are a few of the time bandits. Procrastinating habits steal our time and attention leaving us very little for when we really need it. When people say, "I don't have time!" Is that the truth or is it an excuse to get-out of something they really don't want to do? Learning to be honest with ourselves will help filter out unnecessary tasks and habits, and we'll be less of a nuisance to others.

To do or not to do! Use a time-log to know how well you use your time. Find out what are your time wasters and what chores can others take over from you. Estimate how much time you have control over and understand how much you continue to battle with the 'pending' list. Identify what is urgent vs. important vs. necessary. Prioritise!

In life everything has its own time, place and season. There is a season in which to till the soil, a season in which to plant the seeds, a season in which to reap the harvest or enjoy the fruits of hard work. Most of all be flexible. If things aren't going the way you planned, it's not the end of the world. Hence if you can understand the rhythm of the seasons, you can begin to be more patient with yourself.

It's Time… to realise that I am the master of time; there is no shortage of time. Break the illusion that there will be more time in the future! What I need to do, I need to do now. Don't listen to the internal committee of useless and negative thoughts; take courage, prioritise what is important in your life and take that first step. Once you step onto the boat… the rest is plain cruising and you'll have the time of your life!

Carefree Emperor

Living in a world full of uncertainties, ambiguities and unpredictability can make us pessimists if we are not careful to guard our attitude. Learning to stay carefree and positive has never been more crucial than it is at this time in the world.

Yet how do we strike that fine balance between paying attention and being tension-full? How can we be carefree without becoming care-less?

In fact there is so much to worry about if we think about it: natural calamities, divorce rates soaring, the disastrous state of politics today, and the list goes on. As you see there is ample negativity if we choose to focus on it.

With so much talk of doom looming for humanity, we may feel we just want to hide under the duvet and wake up when it's all over!

Very much like the attitude we create around the glass of water – some think its half full while others think its half empty – so too there are some who are carefree about what is happening to the world, knowing there is something bigger and better coming, while others continue to remain buried in the tragedies. There is good AND bad in the world. What do you choose to focus on and therefore give your energy to?

Some may ask, isn't it natural to be consumed by the negativity that surrounds us? Are we being hard-hearted if we don't succumb to misery as we hear our friends telling us their stories of heartache and hardship? Is that taking the 'art of detachment' too far?

Not really. Imagine that a young man has just been run over in a car accident. There are two other people at the scene. One is the mother, distraught, frantic and despairing. The other is the doctor, an equally caring individual, but detached, calm and efficient. Which one is most able to help the boy, perhaps even save his life?

Getting tangled up in emotions and feelings of fear is not always a good thing. We all want to help others, we all want to help to make the world a better place, but we cannot serve others if we are fearful, depressed, or hiding away in a cupboard.

The last thing that the world needs now is more negativity. So why send your negative vibrations out there just to add to the already overburdened earth?

Instead, the world needs light, it needs peace, and it needs love and these emerge from a carefree state of mind. Do not confuse this with a mind that is careless or irresponsible. You can be carefree when you have wisdom and insight. A wise one will be able to ascertain, discriminate and decide calmly and gracefully. Thus the one who is carefree is like an emperor – one who is unaffected by the negative vibrations and instead is able to charge the atmosphere with positivity and hope.

For a Carefree Emperor, (whether a 'he' or a 'she'!) the

whole point of being on this planet is to share the gifts that we've all been given and so it is not a question of being cold and detached from the world, but the Carefree Emperor sits on a throne of self-respect and gives respect to others. He is a master of his mind, his feelings and emotions. His Mind, Intellect and Subconscious are his ministers and his senses are his subjects.

The Carefree Emperor has the power of his righteous actions as his shadow and not the FBI! He lives on the faith of his past good deeds – knowing that they will protect and serve him. He is neither guilty nor afraid, as he has done nothing wrong.

The Carefree Emperor is one who rises above and beyond the negative forces of the world without even being coloured by a drop of it. From his elevated position he can see and understand the whole picture. He has a heart big enough to embrace the negativity of the world, without judging anything. And the generosity of spirit to give when others just want to take.

Yes, he is detached, but also very loving. From where he sits he can understand the significance of the past and perceive the future and he inspires a positive outcome through the gift of his elevated thoughts and good wishes. He does not give power to what is wrong: he gives power to what is right.

But how to become a Carefree Emperor? Just by knowing and being who I really am. We are greater than we ever imagined, as souls we are all offspring of the one Creator.

Therefore being great is our birthright! Only when we let go of our smallness can we truly be free. Real freedom is knowing and living in the awareness, that we have already been given everything we need to live our lives in the best possible way. We belong to the Highest on High, and so how can we be beggars? Yes, it will take some effort and dedication to reach this elevated state of mind, but it is possible for each of us… we have already been equipped with all the powers, we just need to learn how to use them!

The Carefree Emperor is courageous enough to start a revolution of calm and peace, of tranquillity and love. He takes the first step of courage and forgiveness without expecting others to do so first.

Most of all, the Carefree Emperor has the treasure of happiness in his heart, which in itself is a gift to the world. It is the light that gives others hope.

It's time… to claim your inheritance and become a master of the self. You are here not as a victim, but as a self-sovereign, and you are here to contribute to the sum total of goodness in the world. It's time to stop playing small and to recognise your greatness… to remain carefree and 'careless' – without a care in the world – like a true Emperor!

A Silent Mind

Do you fear silence, or welcome it? Do you find yourself constantly needing chatter, music or TV around you to feel safe and connected? Are you able to be with yourself without being surrounded by noise and action without feeling bored, lonely or depressed?

What if silence became your friend and ally – how would your life be different? When we begin to learn to be at peace with ourselves and the world, then silence is not threatening, empty or devoid of meaning, but it becomes a space where we can nourish and enrich ourselves, where we can grow and blossom. Once we understand what silence truly is, we can begin to have a loving relationship with it and we will never fear being alone or silent again.

Deep silence – as opposed to simply the absence of sound – is the essence of real spirituality. Internal noise and clutter is not only a distraction, but it also creates blocks and barriers that do not allow us to touch our soul, our spirit within. Silence allows us to go inside and connect with that powerful, confident and authentic part of us that is not accessible any other way. It allows us to find ourselves and BE ourselves. And we can also glimpse the many treasures hidden within.

Silence is golden, speech is silver. Silence is deep, words are shallow. In fact we sometimes spoil the moment with words, when silence is the real answer or antidote to the problem. There is a common saying 'an empty vessel makes most noise '. When someone's pot of wisdom and self-respect is full, then it is evident they speak less, and they are listened to more. Those who talk a lot and brag about their wares very often have little self-respect.

Silence is very satisfying, whereas talking and chatter are never ending. As we create the silence of mind, we learn to weigh our words and say only what is necessary. We do not waste words. We listen more than we speak thus we learn rather than lecture. We let go of the need to prove ourselves and replace it with gratitude and appreciation. We cultivate inner strength to deal with whatever comes our way with calmness and assuredness.

A person who is nourished by silence is happy, contented and serene. Just look at the face of the Buddhist monk and you will know that a life of contemplation is indeed a life of joy and freedom.

Silence is also purity. We are captivated by the innocent smile of a small baby, entranced by the simplicity of a mind unencumbered by worldly or mundane thoughts. In silence we are able to appreciate every detail of nature and its majestic beauty quietens our mind.

Silence gives us solutions when too many thoughts often result in confusion. In silence the 'penny drops' and solutions come easily and naturally. When we step away from overthinking about an issue we are able to see the bigger picture, rise above and put it in its proper perspective.

Words give us knowledge, thoughts give us understanding, but only silence can give us an experience. Whether it is in meditation, contemplation or prayer, when our pure thoughts take us into silence, only then can we find our inner world. Only then can we have REAL-EYE-sation that there is a whole realm of experience beyond the physical.

And perhaps this brings us to the most important aspect of all. Silence is that secret, invisible gateway to a profound, loving and fulfilling relationship with The Silent One. Silence is the only way to hear Him.

It's Time… to give yourself the gift of… s i l e n c e …

Slow Down... and Speed Up

It is common knowledge that 'speed kills'. Speeding cars are the leading cause of death in Kuwait (my current homebase). If we all just slowed down a little, perhaps we would not only save lives but also save our souls.

As the pace of the world around us gathers momentum, we may feel the urge to race with it. Everything is getting quicker, faster and supposedly more efficient; online services, deliveries of goods, cars, planes, internet connections, you name it. Yet within the eye of this hurricane there is a calm that we need to capture. We need to learn not to be affected by the storm outside and instead nurture the peace inside.

Check, how many times you find yourself using the words, 'Come on', 'Hurry up!', 'Quick!', 'Faster!', 'Yallah!' (Arabic for let's go) throughout the day. And then to ask yourself, what is the hurry? And after you have done what you needed to, then what, and then what, and then what? Do you see where I am going with this example? What is your destination? Where are you headed? Check that more haste does not create less speed!

We rush in life to finish our studies, so that we may work to earn money, so that we may be successful earlier and retire earlier. We work our butts off for the kids, who too will work their butts off for theirs, and so the cycle continues. So which generation will stop to enjoy the fruits of their labour? It is a sad state of affairs that we get so caught up in the doing, instead of in the being, the 'in-sperience'.

Technology is our friend but also our foe. It was supposed to give us more time to do the things we wanted, to experience more leisure, yet instead it has become a means to consume time as it forces us to speed up our replies and reactions. We find we have become slaves to technology as we respond to every message, bleep, ping and pong. So which is the slave and which is the master? Someone remarked that we were better off in the days when blackberries and apples were just fruits!

To slow down does not mean to be lazy or inactive. Quite the contrary. As we slow down, and give emphasis to our inner world, our thoughts are fewer and more focused. We become happier, more productive, thus we speed up our inner progress.

It's an illusion to think that as I do more, and I do it more quickly, then I will become more, and acquire more. The truth is that I am actually losing. I am taking away from my spirit. I am depleting my spiritual energy, not enhancing it.

How often have we made mistakes in haste that we regretted later? If only we had slowed down a little, or took time to make certain decisions, then our time would be used in a worthwhile way.

As I slow down, focus on what I want and redirect my thoughts, then I am more likely to achieve what I want. Racing or running after things could even push them away from me. As spiritually enlightened beings, we can trust that whatever needs to come to us will arrive in its own time.

Slow down, take in and enjoy this moment right now… and now… and now. The present is the only time I can truly experience. I am perfectly content to be where I am right now.

Learn to slow down by taking in deep breaths through out the day. Check yourself, are you feeling stressed or at peace? Learn to eat slowly, chewing your food well. Walk a little more slowly and observe all the things around you.

You may even like to experiment with a technology-free day or even just a couple of hours, and see what happens.

If you adopt these new habits then you may even find you will accomplish your work in half the time. Limiting the things that cause you stress will help you become a master rather than a servant.

It's Time… to slow down and breathe deeply. Enjoy the present moment and enhance the quality of your life. Tame your technology and become a master of time.

The Mirror Tells No Lies

Did you know that everything you see in others, yes, the good, the bad, and the ugly, is simply a mirror reflection of yourself? For you to be able to recognise a weakness, or see strength in others means that you have to have at least a trace of it in yourself. Otherwise, how could you then recognise it in others? If you want to have successful relationships then you have to take responsibility and ownership for your own thoughts and feelings, this is the key to building inner strength and emotional stability.

At first you may be shocked by the thought that that person who drives you crazy or causes you pain is mirroring back something within you! However, if you truly understand this deep spiritual point, then it can set you free from creating the habit of complaining, blaming and comparing. This firmly puts the ball back in your court. You can no longer play the victim – you need to stand up and take responsibility for what and who you are – it is always easier to point the finger at others. This is a real step towards freedom and self-mastery.

Just as a mirror tells no lies, so 'our judgement' and especially criticism of other people is most interesting, because remember - 'the mirror tells no lies'. The fact that you can recognise ego in others, means that, sorry folks no doubt about it, you must have it in yourself. The fact that you recognise kindness and generosity in another means you too must have applied those very same qualities. At some point in time you have been guilty of the same deeds that you now find yourself condemning.

Every time you find yourself commenting on the actions of others, it would serve you well to take a moment for reflection to check your own actions. And here is another very beautiful point of learning: as you begin to correct yourself, you will see that others begin to change and mirror back the very same correction. If you get irritated and aggressive others will also. However, if you show humility in a situation, most likely others will start to show humility too. Although you may need to be patient before seeing the results!

You have to be willing to recognise your own shortcomings. If you really wish to build up your inner power, then you will see the mirror as a gift that allows you to see yourself and take the necessary steps towards positive change. It takes a great soul to initiate a great act… to forgive… to step back... and give others a chance... to maintain silence instead of shouting back… this new behaviour takes time but also brings great rewards.

Just as a mirror can magnify a light, so too you can light up the life of others by shining brightly yourself. When you choose to see the best in them, by accentuating the positive and seeing the beauty in each soul then your light also shines. By allowing others to see their own truth, beauty and magnificence, then you mirror back to them their pure potential. This is perhaps the greatest service you can do for others because therein lies the healing for each and every soul, to be able to really see the essential goodness that is in each one of us.

When your mirror is dirty you cannot even see the beauty that is right in front of your eyes. What is obscuring your vision? It is the dirt of your own negative vision and attitude that creates waste thoughts and feelings. Negative attitudes and beliefs can only cloud your vision. Release them.

It's Time… to accept that 'the mirror tells no lies'. Remember that the method for your own salvation from old patterns of thinking and finger pointing, the blaming others and everything that goes with it is to simply begin with some small change in your life. Begin by polishing your own mirror, and then reflect out only goodness and without a doubt only goodness can shine back to you.

The Power of Detachment

When people imagine a path of spiritual enlightenment, they sometimes assume it is synonymous with being a recluse. The notion of leading a spiritual lifestyle can invoke images of monks in secluded monasteries or a call for an esoteric lifestyle. Conversely, some may relate it with the culture of the sixties, an era of free expression and non-conformity. So what does it really mean to lead a spiritual life?

In fact, we are all on a spiritual path, whether we realise it or not! We are all spiritual beings, and the purpose of spiritual knowledge is to help one understand and experience themselves as they really are, an original soul, and to re-discover their innate spiritual qualities of peace, love, truth and power. However, knowledge alone is not enough. We also need to take time out to reflect, experience and emerge our true nature. Through the art of meditation one can set these original qualities in motion.

Raja yoga meditation is a universal approach to spiritual awakening and self-development. The word meditation is derived from the Latin word "mederi", which means to heal, to take care of, and to cure. Meditation can certainly be defined as a healing process; healing the mind, body and soul. The connection between the soul and the body is such that dis-ease within our consciousness will also manifest as some type of disease in our physical body. When healing, one needs to mentally step away (detach) from the pain to uncover the causes of physical suffering. For someone on a spiritual path, to go deeper within to understand the root causes buried deep within the consciousness, is the beginning of the healing process.

Detachment then, is a crucial pivot to gain perspective or objectivity in our healing process and it is an avenue to tap into our inner wisdom. Detachment in this sense does not mean to be aloof, cold, or uncaring. At the simplest level detachment means to stand back, that is, to keep some distance between the conscious "I" and our actions or thoughts. To be 'detached' means to be an observer. This attitude of being a 'detached observer' allows us the space to gently and constructively judge, and then transform our feelings and behaviours, thus bringing us into harmony with our innate qualities and allowing an experience of unconditional love.

Imagine your-self standing out at sea in a lighthouse and looking toward the mainland. Or imagine flying high on a two-seater plane over the country, or standing on the top of a cliff looking down at the valley. With this broad, bird's eye view, one can begin to see the bigger picture as one detaches from the details of the situation. We are no longer caught up in the trivialities of everyday life. A heightened level of clarity and calm comes to us without effort. It's possible to appreciate life in a fresh, new and encompassing way.

Real detachment is to involve ourselves in the drama of life and yet not be attached to it. It means to be giving and loving without feeling that we need to take anything. It allows us to receive without the pain of wanting or longing. This fine balance is a state of equilibrium that will take time to acquire, as we gain enough experience to bring maturity, confidence and stability in our lives. But it is not difficult given the right understanding.

Spiritual wisdom tells us that when we attach our consciousness to anything we lose a certain amount of our freedom to it. Try this exercise. Sit in a chair and pretend that the chair symbolises everything you have. Now hold onto the chair as tight as you can, because you can't afford to let go of these attachments, they mean too much to you; they represent all your securities. Are you holding tightly? Now try and move with the chair. Can you do it? Can you do it easily?

When you are sitting in the chair you and the chair are attached. It is controlling you. It is dictating your posture, your comfort, or lack of it; it is restricting your movement. Once you get up and separate yourself from the chair, YOU have power over it and can move it easily where and when you want. You realise you are not the chair nor do you have to carry the burden of it. With objectivity you can put the chair down and distinguish between yourself and the chair, giving yourself the opportunity to make choices and decisions from a place of detachment and freedom.

The same principle applies to relationships. When we are attached to an object or person, they, or it, are in our consciousness: we are attached by an invisible thread. There is a mental bond, an internal link we feel. This is very natural, of course, but when this attachment consumes us, the thread can become like a heavy chain, it can become the seed of fear: fear of loss, damage or change. This fear and insecurity creates life-draining emotions, and attitudes such as anger, envy, jealousy, possessiveness, begin to arise. When these emotions are present, can we love, can we be caring, and can we allow others to love us?

Fear and love are opposite emotions that don't co-exist, like day and night or hot and cold, or winter and summer. The power of detachment fosters and nurtures spiritual love. It releases us from the need to hold on tightly to things or people as we realise we are not our insecurities.

This ancient wisdom has been around for thousands of years. However today, in our modern, busy lifestyles, we don't value looking closely into the inner recesses of our soul. On the contrary, the consumer society encourages us to look outside our selves: buy this; obtain that; achieve the other; appear like this, all in the hope of discovering our real self. From a purely spiritual perspective, attachment is a grievous misuse of our energy and time, especially our attachment to our self-image

The lotus flower is a universal symbol that epitomises the attainment from the power of detachment. It grows in dirty, stagnant water yet it holds its head up high, and brings beauty to the world around it, pure, positive energy. As you involve yourself in the mud of daily living, remember, that you are so much more than that. Even while you are entrenched in situations, detach from the 'doing,' detach from the ego, and awaken your consciousness. Your inner qualities will emerge. Peace will flow through you, and touch all that is around you.

So if you had plans to flee from the drama of life and hibernate in some corner to attain inner peace and love, think again; for that is neither the meaning nor the experience of leading a spiritual life of detachment

It's Time… to experiment with the art of detachment and see how it brings freedom and tranquillity in your life. The extent to which we experience love, self love, and to love those around us is, paradoxically, the extent to which we remain detached, free from negative thoughts … to be the lotus - unaffected by the surroundings, and at the same time an example of beauty, simplicity and dignity.

Slow Down and Stop Rushing

In today's crazy world it's easy to spend a lot of our time rushing from A to B, only to find that those few seconds of haste don't make a significant difference in our day. Rushing around without hardly a minute to spare has become a necessity or even an addiction. In our pursuit of speed, we lose our peace in the soul and create unnecessary adrenalin in the body, which only fatigues the muscles and makes us more tired than productive. Learning to slow down is the key to being more effective!

Imagine a world in which everyone decelerated just a little – drivers, motorcyclists, housewives and executives. For a start there would be fewer accidents! Giving way to others with grace may mean that you will be a few minutes later at the most. Is it really so important that you save a few seconds at the expense of your sanity or blood pressure?

Imagine living your life at a slightly slower pace, and enjoying the moment instead of always frenetically scrambling to what's next.

Very often we jump from one action to the next and forget what we just did or which direction we just came from. We are so heavily consumed in action that we lose awareness of everything around us and consequently we lose the experience of the moment. Then we don't have time to pause, 'smell the roses' or enjoy the moment!

We create for ourselves a vicious cycle. We find ourselves running after time, and as we hurry, we make mistakes, accomplish little and therefore need more time to do the things we need to do!

The key to breaking this vicious cycle is to resist the very thought of haste. To slow down means to step into the present moment, to be alert, conscious and aware. Then as we become focused, we can harness our inner powers and are better able to discern and decide. Instead of simply reacting we can choose the most appropriate responses. It's a change of attitude from feeling out of control to being the master.

And when we sit to reflect at the end of the day we are contented and at peace, knowing that every minute was used in a worthwhile way and to its best advantage. In this way we can honour our daily tasks and responsibilities and sail through them with lightness and ease.

The example of the tortoise and the hare is an excellent one – slow and steady wins the race!

It's Time… to think before you think, think before you speak and think before you act. Taking that little extra time to hold this attention will reap greater dividends in the long run. Become like the tortoise, 'smell the roses' and watch the other hares go by!

What if Important Wasn't So Important?

A sense of importance and urgency may give us an adrenaline rush and a thrill to life, but on the other hand it can also become a cause for stress, or even a heart attack! What if we began to make 'big' things smaller in our minds, and instead of jumping to fulfill them, give them exactly the importance they deserve? Perhaps then we could slow down and begin to live life in the calm lane.

Some people just have the habit of making everything so big and important in their mind that there is no high, average or low activity on their list. It's ALL important! And because of this high demand, and the toll it takes on them, perhaps little actually gets accomplished. These people live in gloom as they notice at the end of their day that everything, that is, 'everything important', has not been completed.

As we become preoccupied in everything so called 'important' and start giving it our undivided attention, we are actually setting ourselves up for defeat, disappointment and sorrow. Why? Because when we say that something is important it means we intend to put our all into it; give it everything we've got. Then we put all our 'eggs in that one basket' so to speak. But what if that basket drops! What if things do not go the way we planned? We only create pain for ourselves.

In fact, nothing is important and yet everything is important! Isn't all of life important? Isn't it important to breathe and to walk and to be able to see? It is only after the advent of life in the fast lane and because of the rise of our desires, goals and ambitions, that we have re-defined the category of 'importance' and what important means – and thereby what we should give our time, money and energy to. But are we getting it right?

What is truly important? Not the dramas that go on 'out there' in life, but the drama that goes on inside of us, in our minds and hearts. If we give importance to the thoughts in our mind then we shall never have to worry, because we will realise that the external is really not as important as we think it is. In the awareness of the internal being, the 'real me', I realise that what goes on out there does not add anything extra to me, to my real importance or to my state of mind. It is what is happening on the inside that is of the utmost importance.

So, what if nothing 'out there' was really as important as we give it credit for? And everything was on a par with each other? Then we would not have biases and preferences, and we would be more relaxed whether something happened or it didn't happen; all is okay! In this way we can keep ourselves light and easy and are able to flow with the drama of life. Isn't this a much more stress-free way of living? When I think of something as important, then I become serious, and stop having fun. I switch into left-brain analytical mode instead of keeping myself light hearted.

If we are living in the body-conscious world, in order to boost our self-respect, we may think that 'I am more important, than this one... this thing, or this situation.' But be careful... this is the ego 'I' speaking. However the

'I' focused in true self-respect, or inner-being awareness, values the self simply because 'I am' and not because of what I have. So in this sense, being is more important than doing. Then I will automatically value myself, my time and other resources.

What else is important? This moment. The now. This is the most important place to be. Don't give importance to the past or the future, otherwise you will find yourself living there! So instead, live the moment.

Next time you find yourself giving importance to something, step back a little and check. Is this really important? Could there be something more important or meaningful that I could be doing with this precious moment? Will it give me the peace and happiness I seek in life?

We are so often exclaiming to ourselves how things are very important and that we have to rush to complete them. So next time exclaim instead: it's NOT so important! And more: 'what really is the most important thing for me to do right now?'

Perhaps the answer will be, 'Just relax and breathe in'! Then let go of whatever it was, or decide to do it at an appropriate time.

It's Time… to reassess what is really important and what is not. Let go of the stress and keep yourself light, easy and happy. Now, isn't that important?

Consistency

Consistency is a virtue. You may not be the number one student at school, but you will certainly get plus points for being steady and constant. Constancy or consistency creates order and discipline in your life that enables you to be stable and strong, firm and certain. But what is the key to this 'constant' success?

People who are non-committal, indecisive or vague and almost always let you down at the very last minute are not very popular! No one wants such friends in their circle. And they will very quickly find that invitations to parties and picnics will soon discontinue if they continue their sloppy ways.

Also isn't constancy a relief, especially when it comes to store opening hours or places of service such as the dry cleaners and the corner shop. They help you to plan and prepare and make your life easy – fewer thoughts are spent wondering or speculating. Imagine if the retailers opened the store only when they felt like it, or on a whim. Chances are they would become insolvent and lose customer goodwill.

In marriage, constancy is fidelity. Knowing that your man is yours (and no one else's!) wins deep respect and commitment and will strengthen the bond and devotion. If you are seeking an intimate relationship, look for a consistency in your partner. If he/she says one thing and does something else, or one day does one thing and the next day the opposite, chances are he/she isn't very trustworthy and might pull the 'Runaway Bride' (or groom) stunt on you!

Whether it comes to work or family relationships, when people are consistent in their behaviour and manner in which they respond to things, there is a safety net and a comfort zone and there are no pop up surprises and hence no anxiety or worry created. We too are prepared to respond appropriately.

Apparently, it's not that difficult to be predictable! Albert-László Barabási, Northeastern University physicist, USA, and his colleagues used data from 50,000 anonymous cell phone users to study human mobility, or where we are and when. Their work reveals that our movements follow a pattern, whether we are homebodies or frequent fliers. "The surprise was that we couldn't find unpredictable people," Barabási laughs. "We are all boring. Spontaneous individuals are largely absent from the population!"

Trust is built with time and regularity; when your thoughts, words and deeds are always in alignment. If you undertake something, complete it without any excuses, even if it costs you a little. If you commit to a person, live up to your commitment – these are the signs of a strong, powerful and committed person. In today's fast paced rat race, where time is of the essence, everyone wants a certain surety and continuity, especially when time and energy goes into planning, organising and soul commitment.

Determination is the key. Once you agree to do something, JUST DO IT. Of course we are discussing positive concepts and ideas here. You could equally be determined about smashing up your neighbour's car as payback for him running his engine idle every morning and disturbing your peace… ooops sleep, but that won't win you good marks in the account of your soul – in fact you will be stripped of them.

You build soul power through consistency. You build integrity and loyalty. You earn other's blessings. Maybe even a promotion too. If you continue to provide a service on a consistent basis, you are one step ahead of others no matter how much your competition grows.

Furthermore you will feel confident with a renewed self-respect. We dislike ourselves the most when we have let ourselves down by not living up to our own expectations.

Consistency in your spiritual practice will also carry you a long way down your spiritual path. Even if it be a few minutes of meditation or positive thinking for a day, or waking up early and practicing mind over matter. Being consistent creates a pattern of discipline and order in your life. There is a natural rhythm that will allow you to create a tempo in your life. A steady coherent order is so important for peace of mind.

Beware to not confuse this type of continuity with monotony. This kind of tedium wears away at the soul, whereas consciously exercised consistency energises the soul. In monotony, I do things as a slave, and in consistency, I am a master, exercising choice at every step. There is a time to introduce change and a time to be consistent.

Consistency can also have another meaning – what our bodies are made of. Our bodies are made up of order and discipline. Take for example the lungs, they respire continually. The heart always beats. Blood continuously flows throughout the body delivering oxygen and antibodies. In fact it is an illness when this pattern is interrupted. As soul beings, we are made up of peace and light. We are light beings. And light is a continuous energy.

It's Time… to be more consistent. Ask yourself why you break the patterns when you do. Have you lost momentum or enthusiasm? Choose a positive action and act on it every day. You will feel the self control through this and experience the real meaning of Raja Yoga, mastery of the self. You will earn love and blessings for your constancy and most of all, because you will need to think less, you will feel a greater peace of mind.

About the Author

Aruna Ladva
Speaker, Author, Meditation Teacher

Aruna Ladva is an accomplished meditation teacher and author. She began her journey at the age of 14, and has spent over three decades studying, teaching and facilitating spiritual self-development.

Aruna is fortunate to have a blend of two cultures - east and west - and feels very much at ease anywhere in the world. Born in Kenya, she was educated in England, lived in Canada, the Middle East and various other countries of the world. However she considers India to be her spiritual home.

Aruna has been instrumental in developing meditation centres in Canada, Turkey, Bahrain and Kuwait. She travels the world as a lecturer, teacher and author, and also facilitates retreats and trainings as well as co-managing self-development projects and initiatives.

As a speaker, her approach is pragmatic and down to earth yet infused with a profound understanding of the emotional, mental and spiritual dimensions of life. She has a positive vision for the future and a passion for life, which she also imparts to the many people she meets around the world.

Aruna is a Certified Negotiator in Conflict Resolution. Her knowledge and understanding of Natural Health is exemplified in her practice and promotion of a vegetarian and almost vegan diet and healthy lifestyle.

Aruna's life and writings are inspired and guided by the teachings of the Brahma Kumaris - www.brahmakumaris.org, with whom she studies the gentle art of Raja Yoga Meditation. She has become a dedicated teacher and an envoy for peace.

You can visit Aruna's blog for more inspiration:
www.itstimetomeditate.org

Or E-mail:
info@itstimetomeditate.org

Aruna's Other Books

It's Time... for Relationships
How spiritual wisdom can bring freedom in relationships

In this thoughtful book, based on her own experiences and inner reflections, Aruna explores the many different relationships we have in our lives, both with others and with ourselves. This book is ideal for those wishing to get to the root of relationship problems.

It's Time... for Change
How making positive changes will enhance your spiritual life

It's Time… for Change is for those seekers of truth who do not want to simply live in denial or sweep issues under the carpet. It is for those who have a compelling desire to look inside more deeply and consciously choose to change. Embrace change!

It's Time... for Self-Empowerment
How spiritual power in your life transforms everything

'It's Time... for Self-Empowerment' is for those who long for personal power, for real and life-changing wisdom. Power and wisdom, that can change the way lives are lived and the way the world works. Empower yourself!

To purchase these publications, go to:

www.inspiredstillness.com

About the Brahma Kumaris

The Brahma Kumaris is a network of organisations in over 100 countries, with its spiritual headquarters in Mt Abu, India. The University works at all levels of society for positive change.

Acknowledging the intrinsic worth and goodness of the inner self, the University teaches a practical method of meditation that helps people to cultivate their inner strengths and values.

The University also offers courses and seminars in such topics as positive thinking, overcoming anger, stress relief and self-esteem, encouraging spirituality in daily life. This spiritual approach is also brought into healthcare, social work, education, prisons and other community settings.

The University's Academy in Mount Abu, Rajasthan, India, offers individuals from all backgrounds a variety of life-long learning opportunities to help them recognise their inherent qualities and abilities in order to make the most of their lives.

All courses and activities are offered free of charge.

For more information:
www.brahmakumaris.org

For Brahma Kumaris publications:
www.inspiredstillness.com

How and Where to Find Out More

SPIRITUAL HEADQUARTERS
PO Box No 2, Mount Abu 307501, Rajasthan, India
Tel: (+91) 2974-238261 to 68
Fax: (+91) 2974-238883
E-mail: abu@bkivv.org

INTERNATIONAL CO-ORDINATING OFFICE & REGIONAL OFFICE FOR EUROPE AND THE MIDDLE EAST
Global Co-operation House, 65-69 Pound Lane,
London, NW10 2HH, UK
Tel: (+44) 20-8727-3350
Fax: (+44) 20-8727-3351
E-mail: london@brahmakumaris.org

REGIONAL OFFICES

AFRICA
Global Museum for a Better World, Maua Close, off Parklands Road, Westlands
PO Box 123, Sarit Centre, Nairobi, Kenya
Tel: (+254) 20-374-3572
Fax: (+254) 20-374-3885
E-mail: nairobi@brahmakumaris.org

AUSTRALIA AND SOUTH EAST ASIA
78 Alt Street, Ashfield, Sydney, NSW 2131, Australia
Tel: (+61) 2-9716-7066
Fax: (+61) 2-9716-7795
E-mail: ashfield@au.brahmakumaris.org

THE AMERICAS AND THE CARIBBEAN
Global Harmony House, 46 S. Middle Neck Road,
Great Neck, NY 11021, USA
Tel: (+1) 516-773-0971
Fax: (+1) 516-773-0976
E-mail: newyork@brahmakumaris.org

RUSSIA, CIS AND THE BALTIC COUNTRIES
Brahma Kumaris World Spiritual University
2, Lobachika, Bldg. No. 2
Moscow – 107140
RUSSIA
Tel: (+7): +7499 2646276
Fax: (+7) 495-261-3224
E-mail: moscow@brahmakumaris.org

For publications visit
Website: www.inspiredstillness.com
E-mail: enquiries@bkpublications.com

Aruna Ladva
Blog: www.itstimetomeditate.org
E-mail: info@itstimetomeditate.org